Kuntres

Ahavat Yisrael

Love of a Fellow-Jew

Translated by
Rabbi Zalman I. Posner
Rabbi Nissen Mangel

Edited by
Rabbi Y. Eliezer Danzinger

KEHOT PUBLICATION SOCIETY
770 Eastern Parkway • Brooklyn, New York 11213

Copyright © 1977
Revised Edition 1998
by
Kehot Publication Society
770 Eastern Parkway / Brooklyn, New York 11213
(718) 774-4000 / FAX (718) 774-2718

Order Department:
291 Kingston Avenue / Brooklyn, New York 11213
(718) 778-0226 / FAX (718) 778-4148
E-Mail: kehot@chabad.org

Library of Congress Cataloging-in-Publication Data
Kuntres Ahavat Yisra'el. English.
Love of a fellow-Jew = Kuntres Ahavat Yisrael / translated
By Zalman I. Posner, Nissen Mangel; edited by Y. Eliezer Danzinger. --
Rev. ed.
82 P.
Includes bibliographical references.
ISBN 0-8266-0458-7 (alk. paper)
1.   Golden rule. 2. Ethics, Jewish. 3. Habad. I. Posner, Zalman I.
II. Mangel, Nissen. III. Danzinger, Y. Eliezer. IV. Title.
BJ1286.G64K86   1998
29B.3'6--dc21   98-6108
                                                       CIP

Cover art: *V'ahavta L'rei'acha Kamocha* by Michel Schwartz

Printed in the United States of America

Table of Contents

Publisher's Foreword
to New English Edition

Rabbi Shmuel of Lubavitch once said, "What good is Chasidus and piety if the main quality—*ahavat Yisrael*—is lacking!?"[1]

To that end, Torah literature in general, and Chasidus in particular, is replete with examples and directives regarding this cardinal precept.

As indicated in the Foreword to the first Hebrew Edition,[2] the Lubavitcher Rebbe, Rabbi Menachem M. Schneerson, in the year 5736 (1976), requested the publication of a short anthology of teachings on the theme of *Ahavat Yisrael*. That year, an English adaptation was also published, translated and edited by Rabbis Zalman I. Posner and Nissen Mangel.

Since this earlier English edition is no longer in print, and there is continued demand for this publication, a newly revised edition is presented.

Appended in this new edition is a translation, by Rabbi Y. Eliezer Danzinger, of Rabbi Yoel Kahn's encyclopedic article on *Ahavat Yisrael*, in *Sefer HaArachim-Chabad*. Though included in the original Hebrew Edition, it was not translated in the first English printing. Also incorporated in

---

1. *HaYom Yom*, p. 77.
2. Translated *infra*.

this publication, are translations of Chapter 32 from *Tanya*, and the relevant portion of Epistle 22 from *Iggeret HaKodesh*, taken from *Lessons in Tanya*,[3] translated by Rabbi Levy Wineberg, and Rabbi Sholom B. Wineberg, respectively.

Lessons in Tanya contains numerous insights by the Rebbe. As such, they are included in this work.

Numerous annotations have been added to the original translations. Additional footnotes have been added as well.

Rabbi Y. Eliezer Danzinger edited this present volume, and Rabbi Yosef B. Friedman prepared it for publication.

Our Sages inform us that the Second Temple was destroyed because of senseless hatred—hatred that was totally groundless and irrational.[4] The remedy for this enmity, taught the Rebbe,[5] is its antithesis—unconditional love. One ought to love another Jew even when one can find absolutely no grounds or reason to do so.

It is the publisher's hope that this new edition of *Kuntres Ahavat Yisrael* will inspire an ever-increasing number of readers to further cultivate this unconditional love for one's fellow Jew.

Kehot Publication Society

11 Nissan, 5758

3. Kehot Publication Society, Brooklyn, NY, 1987.
4. *Yoma* 9b.
5. *Igrot Kodesh*, vol. 4, p. 440.

Foreword to
First English Edition

This booklet is a free translation of the Hebrew (Yiddish) text published by "Kehot" Elul, 5736.

The translations were written by Rabbi Zalman I. Posner and Rabbi Nissen Mangel.

Otzar HaChassidim

Adar 7, 5737
Brooklyn, NY

Foreword to
Hebrew Edition

Upon the instruction of the Rebbe *Shlita*, approaching the luminous day, *Chai Elul*, birthday[1] of the two great luminaries—the Baal Shem Tov, founder of general Chasidus, and the Alter Rebbe, founder of Chabad Chasidus—and approaching the eve of Rosh Hashana, birthday of the Rebbe, the "Tzemach Tzedek," we are privileged to publish this monograph *Ahavat Yisrael*, a short compendium[2] of teachings by these luminaries of Israel, whose light shall guide us until the coming of *Mashiach*. It is particularly apropos at this time since the month of *Elul* is a period of preparation for receiving the blessings of G-d, to be inscribed and sealed for a good year, for which we say, "Bless us our Father, all of us as *one*, in the light of Your countenance," and not when, G-d forbid, there is dissension.

---

1. *Sefer HaSichot 5703*, p. 142, 146; Notes appended to *Sefer HaMa'amarim 5708*, p. 292.
2. See references appended to this monograph: Comments on *Tanya*, chapter 32, and on the *Maamar* of the Tzemach Tzedek. [These comments are not included in this translation]. Also appended, *Sefer HaArachim Chabad*, vol. 1, s.v. *Ahavat Yisrael* [translated in the Appendix of this ed.].

Through the dissemination of their teachings, we hasten the promised coming of *Mashiach*, as described in the famed epistle of the Baal Shem Tov on the subject.[3]

The Rebbe *Shlita* added several annotations and footnotes.

Otzar Hachassidim

Elul 15, 5736
Brooklyn, New York

---

3. *Keter Shem Tov*, beginning.

AHAVAT YISRAEL
Introduction

HALACHA, TORAH LAW

I

Love your fellow like yourself.

Lev. 19:18[1]

II

R. Akiva said, "This is a great principle in the Torah."

Sifra, loc cit.[2]

III

It is a *mitzvah*[3] for every person to love every Jew, just as he loves himself, as it says, "Love your fellow like yourself." Hence, one must speak favorably of another and be consider-

---

1. *Targum Yonatan ben Uziel:* Love your fellow so that what is hateful to you, you will not inflict upon him. See *Shabbat* 31a; Rambam's *Sefer HaMitzvot,* Positive *Mitzvah* 206 (ed. Heller): ". . . for him equally (*kamohu*), and all that I abhor for myself, or for my dear ones, I abhor for him just as much (*kamohu*)." Apparently, in some editions, the sentence between the two *kamohu's* was inadvertently omitted.
2. See also *Yerushalmi Nedarim* 9:4; *Bereishit Rabba* end of *parsha* 24, quoted by *Rashi,* in his commentary on *Lev.* 19:18. For the Chabad interpretation see *Or HaTorah, Chukat,* p. 760, and *Pinchas* p. 1120.
3. Rambam's *Sefer HaMitzvot,* Positive *Mitzvah* 206; *Hilchot Dayot,* 6:3. See there *Hago'at Maymunit* no. 1. Also *Sefer HaChinuch,* section *Kedoshim,* no. 243; *Shabbat* 31a; *Bereishit Rabba,* end of no. 24.

ate of his possessions—just as one is concerned[4] for one's own possessions and is zealous of one's own honor.

Rambam, Hilchot Dayot, 6:3[5]

IV

Love of a proselyte . . . is prescribed by two positive *mitzvot*. The first as a Jew, since a proselyte is included in the category of "fellow [Jew]"; and the second, as a proselyte, for the Torah says,[6] "And you shall love the proselyte." G-d commanded us to love a proselyte just as He commanded us to love Him, as it says,[7] "And you shall love the L-rd your G-d." G-d Himself loves proselytes, as it says,[8] "He loves a proselyte."

Rambam, ibid. 6:4[9]

V

Before[10] a person begins worship in the synagogue, from

---

4. *Pirkei Avot* 2:10, 12; 4:12.
5. See also Alter Rebbe's *Shulchan Aruch, Orach Chaim* 156:5, and references there, fn. 47, 48.
6. *Deut.* 10:19.
7. *Deut.* 6:5.
8. *Deut.* 10:18.
9. "He commanded . . . as He commanded us to love Him": From this we may infer that the same holds true with respect to the *mitzvah*, "And you shall love your fellow man," for the same reasoning applies here too. As to why the Rambam did not write this explicitly—possibly because this is consistent with his general rule to write only what is explicitly stated in Torah, Talmudic and Midrashic sources. (See *Yad Malachi*, rule 2.) With regards to the *mitzvah* concerning a convert, the Rambam himself writes (*Sefer HaMitzvot*, Positive Mitzvah 207), "this has been elucidated in many *Midrashim*."
10. Since the earlier liturgy is "arranged" during the night—*Shaar HaKolel*.

the portion of the *Akeda*[11] onwards, he must accept upon himself the *mitzvah* of "Love your fellow just like yourself," and intend to love every Jew as himself. Through this, his prayer will ascend, combined with all the prayers of Israel. It will be able to ascend Above and bear fruit.

Shaar Hakavanot, beginning

VI
Before worship it is proper to say, "I take upon myself the positive commandment of *Love your fellow like yourself.*"

Alter Rebbe, Siddur, before Ma Tovu[12]

* * *

---

11. See also *Pri Etz Chaim, Shaar Olam HaAsiya*, end of 1; Arizal's *Shulchan Aruch*, beg. of *Hilchot Beit HaKnesset*; Arizal's *Siddur*.
12. For explanation, see *Sefer HaSichot: Summer 5700*, p. 157. *Sefer HaMa'amarim 5709*, p. 99.

THE BAAL SHEM TOV

VII

The Baal Shem Tov declared that *ahavat Yisrael* is the first portal that leads into the courtyards of G-d.

Likkutei Dibburim II, p. 412

VIII

The Maggid of Mezeritch said: The Baal Shem Tov frequently remarked that love of [the children of] Israel is love of G-d. "You are children of the L-rd your G-d."[1] When one loves the Father, one loves the children.

HaYom Yom, p. 81

IX

Rabbi Schneur Zalman of Liadi, the Alter Rebbe, told his son, Rabbi DovBer: Grandfather (the Baal Shem Tov)[2] said that one must exercise self-sacrifice[3] for *ahavat Yisrael*, even for a Jew whom one has never seen.[4]

HaYom Yom, p. 113

---

1. *Deut.* 14:1.
2. [The Alter Rebbe considered the Baal Shem Tov his spiritual "grandfather," as the Baal Shem Tov was the Rebbe of the Maggid, and the Maggid, in turn, was the Alter Rebbe's teacher.
3. See *Likkutei Sichot*, vol. 1, [English rendition] p. 205ff, p. 128.
4. R. Elimelech [of Lizensk] related what he had heard from the Maggid, "Do you know, Melech, what they say in the Heavenly Academy? *Ahavat Yisrael* entails loving the absolutely wicked just as the perfectly righteous." (*Sefer HaSichot: Summer 5700* p. 117).

X

In the early years of his leadership, the Alter Rebbe taught a pithy doctrine, quoted from his teacher the Maggid, who had heard it from the Baal Shem Tov:

Ahavat Yisrael means cherishing another without discrimination, whether the other is learned or untutored. It is to be a love of brothers,[5] expressed in embrace and osculation,[6] just as love of Torah is demonstrated in the way that its cover is treasured.

Sefer HaMa'amarim 5708, p. 192

XI

We have a tradition from the Baal Shem Tov:

R. Moshe Cordovero's *Tomar Devora*, ch. 2: Accustom yourself to instill the love of all people in your heart, even the wicked, as though they were your brothers and more so, until you implant the love of all people in your heart, loving even the wicked in your heart. Say to yourself, "If only these people would be righteous and repent! So that they would all be great and acceptable to G-d"; as Moshe *Rabbeinu*, who loved all Israel faithfully, declared: "If only all G-d's people were prophets . . ."

Seder Hadorot, year 5372 (from *Sefer Charedim*): "Two great sages, Kabbalists, lived in our generation. R. Moshe Cordovero was the chief magistrate of the *Beit Din* of the Tzfat community, and died in the year 5330. The Arizal, who accompanied his bier, testified that he perceived two columns of fire escorting R. Moshe. We know that this is visible to but one or two in a generation (*Vayakhel Moshe* 7d)." Moreover, this was in the generation of R. Moshe Cordovero!

5.   The special quality of brotherly love is that it endures and is not subject to change. See *Likkutei Torah*, beg. of *Behar*, etc.

6.   Engendered by the love in the depths of the heart, beyond articulation, it cannot be expressed in words but in osculation (*Torah Or*, end of *Truma*. See also *Likkutei Torah*, beg. of *Shir HaShirim*).

When one hears something disparaging about another Jew, even a stranger, one should be sorely distressed, since somebody must be grievously at fault. If the derogatory account is true, then the subject is wrong. On the other hand, if it is false, then the talebearer is in an unenviable situation.

HaYom Yom, p. 112

XII

A tradition from the Baal Shem Tov:

Whoever judges another, favorably or critically, is actually rendering judgment over himself. For example, if someone remarks that so-and-so's good deed or good words deserve G-d's blessings for his needs, or that so-and-so's misdeed or improper speech have earned him punishment, these very remarks are transposed into a verdict about himself, whether favorable or otherwise. Whoever rationalizes an other's suffering instead of agonizing over it, and does not pray for the other's relief, then his own deeds and words are scrutinized [from Above]. By contrast, he who empathizes with his fellow's anguish and prays for him, he will be rewarded.

HaTamim VII, p. 104

XIII

The Alter Rebbe quoted the Maggid, who quoted the Baal Shem Tov:

"Love your fellow like yourself"[7] is an interpretation and exposition of "Love the L-rd your G-d."[8] He who loves a

---

7. *Lev.* 19:18.
8. Deut. 6:5.

fellow Jew loves G-d, for he contains within himself a part of G-d Above. Love for him, for his inward self, is love of G-d.[9]

HaYom Yom, p. 78

XIV

The Alter Rebbe promulgated a teaching of the Maggid in the name of the Baal Shem Tov:

Love of a fellow Jew is a Biblical commandment. Every *mitzvah* has both its positive and negative form. Here, too, "Love your fellow"[10] is the positive facet, and "Do not hate your brother"[11] is the negative.[12] The simplicity of the ordinary Jew, his prayer, his saying of *Tehillim* (Psalms) after

---

9. To amplify from a teaching by the Maggid (*Ohr Torah* on Psalms) on the verse "Do not enter into judgement with us": for all who pronounce judgment on the Jewish people are, in fact, rendering judgement on G-d, for He is united with us.
10. *Lev.* 19:18.
11. *Lev.* 19:17.
12. An openly displayed hatred towards someone is not a violation of this command but a transgression against "Do not take revenge or harbor a resentment" (*Chinuch* no. 238). Nonetheless, the prohibition cited in our text is "Do not hate." This might be explained:
    1. according to *Rambam*, [*Yad HaChazaka*], *Deyot*, 6:5, though the conclusion there specifically limits the scope of "Do not hate" to feelings in the heart. See also end of ch. 7, similar to *Chinuch*;
    2. because "Do not hate" is a logical [psychological] antecedent and cause for "Do not take revenge or harbor a resentment";
    3. he, [the author] may subscribe to the opinion expressed in the *Kesef Mishna's* commentary on *Rambam* [*Yad HaChazaka*] that the prohibition against expressed hatred is included in "Do not hate." The dispute of scholars in later generations concerning this commentary of the *Kesef Mishna* and its apparent contradiction with the Rambam's *Sefer HaMitzvot*, negative commandment 302, is known.

prayer, his performing a *mitzvah* because G-d told us to—these engender delight Above.

Sefer HaMa'amarim 5708, **p. 190**

XV

The worldwide Jewish community is aware of the level of *ahavat Yisrael* that the Baal Shem Tov instilled into the Jewish people through the well-known teaching:

One should love and cherish the very simple Jew, just as one does the greatest scholar, because he is a Jew, and all have one Father, as it is written, "You are children to the L-rd your G-d,"[13] and it is said, "I love you, says the L-rd."[14]

Sefer HaMa'amarim 5708, **p. 79**

XVI

The Greatness of a Jew

A simple Jew is as eminent in his essential, intrinsic quality as the very greatest scholar. It is written, "You are children to the L-rd your G-d,"[15] and it is written, "These are the progeny of Isaac, the son of Abraham; Abraham begot Isaac"[16]—the image of the son was like the image of the father.[17] This is the meaning of the verse, "You are children of the L-rd your G-d": the image of the children, Israel, being compassionate, bashful, benevolent, is like that of their Father, the Holy One, blessed be He, who is merciful, gra-

---

13. *Deut.* 19:17.
14. *Malachi* 1:2.
15. *Deut., ibid.*
16. *Gen.* 25:19.
17. *Rashi, ad loc.*

cious, and abounding in forgiveness to those who repent. Just as He, may He be blessed, is eternal and His Torah and *mitzvot* are eternal, so is His people and heritage eternal. The smallest in Israel is a crown of beauty to "the L-rd, Who is great and highly praised."[18]

Love of a Fellow Jew

Love of a fellow Jew, according to the teachings of the Baal Shem Tov, is not due *only* because every Jew must strive to attain qualities of goodness and kindness. Namely, to rid oneself of the evil traits of conceit, falsehood, jealousy, hatred, and the like, and to acquire the virtuous traits of fear of G-d, love of Torah, cherishing *mitzvot*, humility, truth, love of humanity. All these qualities are included in the three general virtues identified by our Sages [as being characteristic of the Jewish people]: compassionate, bashful, and benevolent.[19]

Rabbi Shlomo Bay'ever related to his father the Baal Shem Tov's interpretation of the Talmudic statement: This nation (Israel) is marked by three character traits: compassion, bashfulness, and benevolence. *Compassion*—a Jew has compassion upon *the neshama* (soul) which has descended from its lofty station. The soul stands before G-d in the *Garden of G-d*, then descends through "hidden stages," to be invested in a [physical] body whose origin is dust and which reverts to dust.[20] *Bashfulness*—they are abashed before the Divine Light that shines over their heads, and improve

---

18. *Psalms* 48:2.
19. *Yevamot* 79a.
20. Cf. Gen. 3:19.

their behavior through the performance of the *mitzvot*. *Benevolence* — the soul of the Supernal Being,[21] sitting upon the "likeness of the Throne," teaches them to [show kindness to their body. To do so by] elevating it and all its needs, as well as their share in the world, as Divine Providence ordains in place and time, to refine and illuminate them with the light of Torah and the service of G-d.

All this is as far as the acquisition of virtuous traits is concerned. However, the love of a fellow Jew is something infinitely more profound.

Rabbi Shlomo related the declaration of the Baal Shem Tov in one of his holy discourses:

"I call as my witness Heaven and Earth [to attest to the following]! The Heavenly Court was adjudicating a case involving a man against whom was laid a serious charge. This man was so simple that he only knew how to pray and recite *Tehillim*. He was exceptional, however, in his love of a fellow Jew, with all the faculties of his soul. In thought, always thinking thoughts of love of a fellow Jew; in speech, speaking of love of a fellow Jew; in deed, benefiting everyone to the best of his ability, sharing the sorrow of every Jew, man or woman, and rejoicing in their joy. The verdict handed down by the Heavenly Court was that this man was to be granted a place among the righteous scholars whom our Sages said were lovers of Israel."

The sigh of a Jew over the suffering of another Jew breaks all the barriers erected by the Accusers. The joy and goodwill

---

21. *Ezekiel* 1:26.

that one feels, and the blessings that one gives, on account of an other's happiness, is as acceptable to G-d as the prayer of Rabbi Yishmael, the High Priest, in the Holy of Holies.[22]

Sefer HaSichot 5703, **p. 161**

* * *

---

22. Cf. *Berachot* 7a.

Rabbi Schneur Zalman of Liadi
The Alter Rebbe

XVII

Love of G-d and love of Israel are equally engraved on the *neshama, ruach and nefesh*[1] of every Jew. It is an explicit passage in Torah: *I love you, says the L-rd.*[2] Love of Israel is so great, for one loves whom the Beloved loves.

HaTamim IV, p. 44-45

XVIII

It is written: "Love the L-rd your G-d with all your heart and with all your soul and with all that you possess"[3]—and even so, G-d forgoes love of G-d , and prefers the love for a fellow Jew.

Sefer HaSichot 5702, p. 15

XIX

"Love the L-rd your G-d." Love of Israel[4] is a means through which to achieve love of G-d. The Mitteler Rebbe,

---

1. These terms describe different stages of the soul, the intellectual, the emotive, and the active. Every person has all of them, but one is dominant, the other dormant.—Translator.
2. *Malachi* 1:2.
3. *Deut.* 6:5.
4. In *HaTamim IV*, p. 45: The "Tzemach Tzedek", Rabbi Menachem Mendel, quoted Rabbi Schneur Zalman: "Love your fellow" is a means to achieve "Love the L-rd your G-d" . . . Since in reference to love of G-d the Alter Rebbe explains that the commandment is to meditate deeply and the love is a consequence and product of medi-

Rabbi DovBer, commented on this teaching of his father: *Ahavat Yisrael* was implanted within (his disciples) even unto their smallest fingernail.

Ibid., p. 15

XX

There is the love of G-d, the love of Torah and the love of Israel. Each of these three types of love has three levels: with all your heart, with all your soul, and with all that you possess. Of the three, *ahavat Yisrael* is supreme, for it includes them all. Whoever has *ahavat Yisrael* inevitably has the love of Torah and the love of G-d, too. But if one has love of G-d, one may still, conceivably, lack the love of Torah. And if one has the love of Torah, he might well lack love of Israel.

Sefer HaSichot 5705, p. 120

* * *

---

tation, then it is quite obvious that this applies as well to love of Israel. Namely, that it comes as a result of deeply pondering the other person's quality. (On Rabbi Schneur Zalman's dictum to meditate deeply, see *HaTamim, ibid.,* also *Mitzvat Ahavat Yisrael* in *Derech Mitzvotecha* of the "Tzemach Tzedek," *infra,* and *Shnei HaMe'orot* vol. 2, par. 2, by the famed Chasid and Gaon, R. Yitzchak Eizik Epstein of Gomel).

XXI
TANYA
Chapter Thirty-Two

Acting on the advice mentioned above—to view one's body with scorn and contempt, and to find joy in the joy of the soul alone—is a direct and easy path toward fulfilling the *mitzvah*, "You shall love your fellow as yourself,"[1] with regard to every Jew both great and small—[in spiritual stature].

Since his body is despised and loathsome [he will not love himself on account of his body more than he loves his fellow; and] as for the soul and spirit, [the differences between his own soul and that of his fellow surely will not diminish the love between them]. For who can know their [the soul and spirit's] greatness and excellence in their source and root—the living G-d?

Furthermore, they are actually all equal;[2] [and not only equal yet separate, but, furthermore] they all have one father.

---

1. *Lev.* 19:18.
2. Note the discrepancy: In speaking of the souls of Israel in general, the Alter Rebbe first writes, "Who can know [can distinguish] their greatness and excellence?", implying that there are in fact differences between one soul and another; here he writes, "They actually are all equal."

   The explanation: As discussed in *Tanya* chapter 2, the original source of all souls is the *Sefirah* of *Chochmah* in the World of *Atzilut*. On this level, all the souls are indeed one entity.

   This is indicated in the words, "They all have one father"—"father" (*Abba*) being the kabbalistic term for *Chochmah*.

   From this source, the souls progress downward through the various *Sefirot* and Worlds. It is this descent that creates differences between souls; one soul is more strongly affected by the descent, and

It is because of this common root in the One G-d that all of Israel are called "brothers"—in the full sense of the word,[3] only the bodies are distinct from each other.

Therefore, there can be no true love and fraternity between those who regard their bodies as primary and their souls secondary, but only a love based on an external factor.

This explains Hillel the Elder's statement concerning the fulfillment of this *mitzvah*: "This is the entire Torah, the rest is but commentary."[4]

For the basis and root purpose of the entire Torah is to elevate and exalt the soul high above the body, to [G-d,] the root and source of all worlds, and also to draw down the infinite light of *Ein Sof* into the Community of Israel—as will be explained further.[5] Meaning, into the fountainhead of

---

another less so. The first stage in this descent is the *Sefirah* of *Binah* in the World of *Atzilut*; thus, it is at the level of *Binah* that the differences between souls first appear.

This is alluded to in the words, "Who can know their greatness and excellence in their source and root—the living G-d?"; in kabbalistic terminology, "the living G-d" is a reference to the level of *Binah* in the World of *Atzilut*.

Speaking of the souls at this level, the Alter Rebbe therefore says that feeling superior to one's fellow is unjustified, because "who can know their greatness and excellence...?"

There are indeed differences between souls—but who knows them? When speaking of the souls having "one father," however, he writes, "they are all equal."

3. From a note by the Rebbe, Rabbi Menachem M. Schneerson: And not only figuratively, in the sense of "relatives" or "similar in appearance" and the like. (The two alternative meanings of "brothers" appear in the commentary of Rashi on *Gen.* 13:8.)

4. *Shabbat* 31a.

5. Ch. 41.

the souls of all Israel, so that "the One [G-d] will reside within [Israel—but only insofar as they are] one," [i.e., united].

But this [indwelling of the light of *Ein Sof* in the Community of Israel] is impossible if there is disunity between the souls, G-d forbid, for "G-d does not dwell in an imperfect [fragmented] place."[6]

Accordingly, we say in our prayers: "Bless us, our Father, all as one with the light of Your Countenance."[7] [This indicates that "the light of G-d's Countenance" can be revealed only when we are united *all as one*] as explained elsewhere at length.

As for the Talmudic statement that if one sees his friend sinning, he should hate him, and should also relate the fact to his teacher so that he too will hate him,[8]—[how does this conform with what was said above]?

This applies only to one's companion [one's equal] in the study of Torah and the observance of the *mitzvot*.[9]

He has also fulfilled with him—[with the sinner]—the injunction, "You shall repeatedly rebuke your friend."[10]

---

6. Cf. *Zohar I*, 216b.
7. Liturgy, final blessing in the *Amidah*.
8. Cf. *Pesachim* 113b.
9. From a note by the Rebbe, Rabbi Menachem M. Schneerson: In other words, the sinner in question is a Torah-observant scholar, but has lapsed in this one instance. In this case his sin is much more severe than usual, since it is written that even the inadvertent misdeeds of a scholar are as grave as deliberate sins. [See *Lessons in Tanya*, vol. 1, p. 426, for an analysis of the Rebbe's note.]

    But even this general assumption of the gravity of his conduct is not sufficient cause to hate him, as the Alter Rebbe continues. Yet, another condition must first be satisfied.
10. *Lev.* 19:17.

[The word used here for "your friend" (*amitecha*) also indicates[11]]—"him who is on a par with you in the Torah and the *mitzvot*,"[12] as it is written in *Sefer Charedim*.[13]

[At this point there is no need to exaggerate the gravity of his sin: it is clearly a deliberate transgression].

However, as to one who is not his companion—[his equal]—in the Torah and the *mitzvot*,[14] nor is he on intimate terms with him[15]—then on the contrary. Of such a situation Hillel said, "Be one of the disciples of Aharon, loving peace and pursuing peace, loving *creatures* and drawing them near to the Torah."[16]

This means that even those who are far from G-d's Torah and His service, for which reason they are classified simply as "creatures"—[indicating that the fact that they are G-d's creations is their sole virtue—even those] one must attract with strong cords of love.

---

11. *Shevuot* 30a.
12. A play on the word עמיתך: עם-אתך. See *Kitzurin VeHaorot LeTanya*, p. 36.
13. By Rabbi Eliezer Azkari (16th century).
14. So that (as our Sages say concerning the ignorant, in general) even his deliberate transgressions are regarded as inadvertent acts, since he is unaware of the gravity of sin.
15. Not only is one not enjoined to hate him: on the contrary, he must in fact, strive to become closer to him, as the Alter Rebbe states shortly. To hate such a sinner is surely unjustifiable, since no sin that he commits is considered deliberate. There is also no reason to keep one's distance from him out of fear that he will learn from his evil ways (in fulfillment of the exhortation of the *Mishnah*, "Do not fraternize with a wicked man"), since he is not on close personal terms with him in any case.
16. *Avot* 1:12.

Perhaps thereby, one will be able, after all, to draw them close to the Torah and the service of G-d.

And even if one fails [in this], he has not forfeited the merit of the *mitzvah* of neighborly love [which he has fulfilled by his efforts in this direction.

Furthermore], even those whom one is enjoined to hate—for they are close to him, and he has rebuked them but they still have not repented of their sins—one is obliged to love them too.

And both [the love and the hatred] are truthful [emotions in this case]. The hatred is on account of the evil within them, while the love is on account of the good hidden in them, which is the divine spark within them that animates their divine soul.[17]

One must also arouse compassion on [the divine soul of the sinner], for in the case of the wicked it is in exile within the evil of the *sitra achra*, which dominates it.

---

17. For this spark of G-dliness is present even in the most wicked of one's fellow Jews; it is merely hidden.

   One may now be faced with the anomaly of a fellow-Jew whom he must both love and hate. However, what attitude should he adopt toward the person as a whole who possesses both these aspects of good and evil?

   When, for example, the sinner requests a favor of him, should his hatred dictate his response, or his love?

   The Alter Rebbe goes on to say that one's relationship, as a whole, with the sinner should be guided by love. By arousing one's compassion for him, one restricts one's own hatred so that it is directed solely at the evil within the sinner, not at the person himself.

Compassion banishes hatred and arouses love—as is known from the verse,[18] "Jacob, who redeemed Abraham."[19]

([20]As for the statement by King David, peace upon him: "I hate them with a consummate hatred,"[21] [reserving no love for them whatsoever], this refers only to [Jewish] heretics and atheists who have no part in the G-d of Israel, as stated in the Talmud, beginning of chapter 16 of Tractate *Shabbat*.)[22]

* * *

---

18. *Isaiah* 29:22.
19. "Jacob" represents compassion, and "Abraham," love. When "Abraham," love, must be "redeemed," i.e., brought out of conceal-ment, it is "Jacob," compassion that accomplishes this redemption; for as said, compassion banishes hatred and arouses love.
20. Parentheses are in the original text.
21. *Psalms* 139:22.
22. Any sinner who is not, however, a heretic, must not be hated with "a consummate hatred," for the *mitzvah* of *ahavat Yisrael* embraces him as well.

XXII

IGGERET HAKODESH

End of Epistle Twenty-Two

. . . Rather, every one should believe with absolute faith in the precept of our Sages, of blessed memory: "And be humble of spirit before every man,"[1] without exception.[2] For it is a true statement and a correct adage that every man becomes better through his fellow.

---

1. Avot 4:10.
2. In Tanya chapter 30, this same teaching of the Sages (a) is not introduced by an injunction that one "believe [in it] with absolute faith"; (b) it is followed by a consideration of the conduct of others.

    Concerning these differences the Rebbe, Rabbi Menachem M. Schneerson, notes:

    Chapter 30 speaks of man's service with regard to himself—his battle with the evil inclination and his efforts to refrain from evil and to do good, and so on. This demands the kind of meditation outlined there, that will lead to proper thought, speech and action—a detailed consideration of the conduct of another individual, who is less righteous, [and yet whose divine service one has to learn to regard as being in fact superior to one's own].

    Belief plays no part in this; all that matters there is that one's mind should compel him to conduct himself as he ought.

    Here, however, in Iggeret HaKodesh, our text speaks of the need to become one with every other Jew—all of us like actually one man. The Alter Rebbe, therefore, has to make provision for the possibility that if one individual imagines a flaw in another or in a group of people, he should not think about it, etc., as is soon stated. Rather, he should believe in this teaching of the Sages.

    Indeed, in order for it to be truly internalized he should believe in it "with absolute faith," and certainly not contemplate the details of the conduct of this individual or the other.

Thus, too it is written,[3] "All the men of Israel . . .
associated together like one man."

Just as one man is composed of many limbs and when
they become separated this affects the heart, for from it there
issues life, therefore, by our truly being all like one man, the
service [of G-d] in the heart [i.e., prayer] will be firmly established. And from the affirmative [you may infer the
negative].[4]

That is why it is said,[5] "To serve Him with one purpose."[6]

Therefore, my beloved and dear ones, I beg repeatedly.
Let each of you exert yourself with all your heart and soul to
firmly implant in your heart a love for your fellow Jew. In the
words of Scripture, "let none of you consider in your heart
what is evil for his fellow."[7]

Moreover, [such a consideration] should never arise in
one's heart [in the first place]. If it does arise, one should
push it away from his heart[8] "as smoke is driven away," as if it
were an actual idolatrous thought. For to speak evil [of
another] is as grave as idolatry and incest and bloodshed.[9]

And if this be so with speech, [then surely thinking evil
about another is even worse].[10] For all the wise of heart are

---

3. *Judges* 20:11.
4. *Sifrei, Eikev* 11:19.
5. *Zephaniah* 3:9.
6. Literally, "with one part" or "with one shoulder": only when all Jews
    fully unite in this way can it be said that they "serve Him."
7. *Zechariah* 8:17.
8. *Psalms* 68:3.
9. *Arachin* 15b.
10. The bracketed words are euphemistically omitted in the Hebrew
    original, and merely hinted at by "etc."

aware of the greater impact [on the soul] of thought over speech, whether for the good or for the better.

* * *

Rabbi Menachem Mendel of Lubavitch The "Tzemach Tzedek"

XXIII
Derech Mitzvotecha
Mitzvat Ahavat Yisrael

The 238th *mitzvah* [in the enumeration of the 613 *mitzvot* of the Torah][1] is to harbor no enmity toward one's fellow, as it is written: "You shall not hate your brother in your heart."[2] The 243rd *mitzvah* is to love every Jew, as it is written: "Love your fellow man as yourself."[3]

The adage of Hillel the Elder to the would-be proselyte, "What is hateful to you, do not inflict upon your fellow man; this is the entire Torah, the rest is but commentary"[4]—is well-known, but not quite clear. Though we can understand that this *mitzvah* is the essence of precepts between man and his fellow, how can it be said with respect to those between man and G-d? Especially in light of the verse, "If you act righteously, what do you give Him?"[5]

---

1. *Sefer HaChinuch.*
2. *Lev.* 19:17.
3. *Ibid.* 19:18.
4. *Shabbat* 31a.
5. *Job* 35:7.

It is also written[6] that it is proper to say before [the morning] prayer, "I hereby accept upon myself to fulfill the positive *mitzvah, Love your fellow man as yourself*"—for it is an all-important principle in the service of G-d. [The following exposition will enable us] to understand the meaning of this *mitzvah*.

I.

[The student of the Arizal [R. Chaim Vital,] writes [in the name of his mentor] in *Sefer Taamei HaMitzvot*, section *Kedoshim*, "All Israel comprises one complete entity within the soul of Adam. As we have stated elsewhere (*Sefer HaGilgulim* 1:2), each individual Jew constitutes one particular part [of Adam's soul]. This is the basis of the responsibility of one Jew for another if he sins.[7] Accordingly, it was the custom of the Arizal to recite the specific transgressions enumerated in the *Vidui* (Confession)[8] [although he did not, G-d forbid, transgress]; for all Israel is one entity."

Meaning, [the soul of] Adam was the general, all encompassing soul of all the souls of Israel (except those which will descend after the time of the Resurrection, see *ibid.*, ch. 7).

---

6. *Siddur Nusach Ha'Ari*, before the beginning of the *Shacharit* Prayer; *Pri Etz Chaim*, "*Shaar Olam HaAsiyah*", ch. 1; *Shaar 3*, end of ch. 2; beginning of *Shaar HaKavanot*.
7. *Sanhedrin* 27b; *Shevuot* 39b.
8. "We have sinned . . . we have robbed, etc.", recited after *Shemoneh Esrei*.

He comprised [within his soul] all the souls, some originating in his head, others in his arms,[9] etc.

For this reason he was called Adam—which is [etymologically] related to *Adameh l'Elyon*, "I will be likened to the One Above."[10] For he was all-encompassing and derived from *Adam de-l'Eila* (Supernal Being)[11] who comprises the Ten *Sefirot* in what is known as *partzuf*. As it is written, "My first-born son Israel,"[12] [and just as a son resembles his father—so Israel (Adam) resembles *Adam de-l'Eila*].

Elsewhere it is explained [in the exposition of the Zoharic statement, section *Yitro*, "All days receive their blessing . . ."] that *Adam de-l'Eila* corresponds to the Divine Name [whose numerical value is] forty-five מ״ה[13] of [the world of] *Tikkun*.[14] This causes the mutual inclusiveness of each of the Ten *Sefirot*—*chesed* contains *gevurah*, *gevurah* contains *chesed*, and so on.

In [the world of] *Tohu*, however, the *Sefirot* were in a state of separation and disunity. The integration of the *Sefirot* [in *Tikkun*] is effected through the Divine Name מ״ה of *mitzchah* [permeating the *Sefirot*]. This is the *Ein Sof* [the

---

9. The soul contains 613 powers and vitalities corresponding to the 613 physical parts of the body. See *Tanya*, Part 1, ch. 51. It is to this spiritual *head* and *arms* that is being referred here.
10. *Isaiah* 14:14.
11. Based on *Ezekiel* 1:26.
12. *Exodus* 4:22.
13. The four letters of the name *Havaye* may be "spelled" in four different ways. Each spelling yields a different numerical value. The numerical value of *Hava'ye* when spelled out thus יו״ד ה״א וא״ו ה״א is 45 or מ״ה.
14. I.e., the world of *Atzilut*.

Infinite] who comprises all the worlds and realms, as well as all the individual beings, as it is written, "All things come from You."[15] Hence, it brings about their coalescence even after they each have emerged into their particular revealed aspects. This is the meaning of what is written in *Tikkunei Zohar*,[16] "The Name מ״ה is the path of *Atzilut*," for just as a path joins two separate places [so the Name מ״ה binds the *Sefirot* one with the other]. See there for a detailed explanation.

Similarly, it can be understood how the souls of Israel collectively comprise one complete entity, viz., the soul of Adam, which is the general, all-embracing [soul]. Although it contains 248 distinct [spiritual] parts, nevertheless, these parts are mutually inclusive, each containing the others.

By way of analogy, a human body consists of various parts: head, feet, hands, nails, etc., yet each part incorporates all the others. In the hand, there flows something of the foot's vitality through the interconnecting veins. The same is true of all the other bodily parts. Therefore, as is known, it is possible to cure one part of the body by an injection into another part, because of the confluence of blood in the circulatory system.

This integration of the bodily organs and of the vital forces within them is due to the general life-force that comprises them all. This general life-force dwells[17] in the brain

---

15. *Chronicles* I, 29:14.
16. Introduction.
17. Literally, irradiates.

whence it is diffused and individualized,[18] but contains them all. (As for example, the unformed hylic matter, "hyle")

For this reason the brain perceives the pain of all the 248 organs, and [to the brain] the pain of the arm and of the leg are similar. Indeed, at times the brain senses more acutely the pain of a wound to the nail than the pain of a wound to the hand, as can be observed.

Similarly, the coalescence of the 248 parts of Adam's soul, one with the other, is due to the source of his soul's vitality deriving from the Supernal Wisdom of the Supernal Being, the blessed *Ein Sof.* G-d abides in, and is united with, His Wisdom, for "He and His Wisdom are all one."[19]

Therefore, it is written, "My first-born son." Just as a son is derived from a drop deriving from his father's brain [so, too, his soul is derived from His Wisdom].[20] However, after Adam's soul was divided into numerous root-souls, which in turn were subdivided into manifold branches and *sparks* in individual bodies, the soul's state is analogous to bodily organs which have become severed one from the other. In this state, the pain of the foot is no longer felt by the hand.

But the separation [between one Jew and another] exists only in respect to the body. As parts of a comprehensive whole, their souls are never truly separated, analogous to a hand that has veins linking it to the legs and eyes, and the foot to the hand. Accordingly, the hand, for example, feels an intense pain, in a spiritual sense, from the pain of the eye, as mentioned above.

---

18. See *Tanya*, Part 1, ch. 51.
19. *Hilchot Yesodei HaTorah 2:10. Cf. Tanya*, Part 1, ch. 2.
20. Cf. *Tanya, loc cit.*

Hence, the Arizal would recite confession (*vidui*) for all the transgressions that any Jew may have committed. For the part [in the General Soul] in which that Jew's soul was rooted, was suffering, and this pain was transmitted to the higher parts where the soul of the Arizal was rooted. How much more so is this true with respect to the Source of our souls, i.e., "the brain of the Father and His blessed Wisdom"[21] which comprises all the 248 parts, and perceives their discomfort.

We are therefore commanded to love every individual Jew, since each one includes all the souls of Israel, as in the above analogy of the bodily organs. Thus, a person incorporates also his fellow, so he should love his fellow as he does himself. Similarly, he is incorporated within his fellow, as mentioned above with reference to the interconnection of the body's organs.

For this reason also one must accept upon himself this *mitzvah* before beginning to pray. One is thereby able to offer one's soul to G-d in [the recital of the word] *Echad* [one—in *Keriat Shema*] so that it rise before Him in the manner of *mayim nukvin* in *Keriat Shema*. This elevation can be achieved only when the soul is complete and "healthy." Namely, when it unites with all the souls—just as a bodily organ is healthy when its veins that link it to all the organs are healthy. Then [his soul] can ascend in favor before G-d in His blessed Wisdom, which contains all the souls actually as one. Inasmuch as his soul is also unified with all others, it

---

21. Cf. *Tanya, loc. cit.*

can ascend into the general, all encompassing Light that is its source and root.

This unity is achieved when a man demonstrates his unreserved love for his fellow—as the interconnection of the bodily organs one with the other—[with a feeling of] "what is mine is yours"[22] for he is his "bone and flesh."[23] If, however, he feels enmity in his heart for a fellow Jew, he sunders from his soul that part of his fellow contained within him, rejecting him by this hatred and removing his will from him.

He thereby blemishes and mars his own soul, for now this part is lacking in him. He thus becomes defective—since every individual part is comprised of all the 613, and through his hatred, he severs from himself that individual part. He is then unable to ascend in favor before G-d; as it is written: "He who has a blemish shall not approach to offer. . . "[24] For the *Or Ein Sof,* blessed is He, Who comprises them all, will not tolerate him because of the flaw within him, being deficient of that individual—for the *Or Ein Sof* comprises that missing individual as well. This should suffice for the intelligent.

That is why we have been commanded with several prohibitions against the offering by blemished *Kohanim* and against defective sacrifices themselves, as they are described in the portion *Emor.*[25] We have likewise been enjoined with a positive precept to offer every sacrifice unblemished, as it is

---

22. *Avot* 5:10.
23. Cf. *Genesis.* 29:14.
24. *Leviticus.* 21:17.
25. *Ibid.* 22:17 ff.

written, "To be accepted, it shall be perfect; it shall have no
blemish."[26]

II.

We have clearly elucidated the reason for this *mitzvah* [of
ahavat Yisrael]. Yet, based upon an exposition of the above-
mentioned statement of Hillel, there is another wonderful
explanation. It, too, elucidates the profound goodness that
one accomplishes for himself and for the entire world
through observing this positive *mitzvah*. It also explains the
opposite, G-d forbid, when one neglects it and transgresses
the negative injunction of the Torah, "You shall not hate."

Let us understand why Hillel paraphrased this *mitzvah* in
the negative: *What is hateful to you do not do to your fellow*,
and did not state it in the positive, as did Onkelos in his
rendition: *Love your fellow as yourself*. For in this way Hillel
interpreted this *mitzvah* in a deeper sense, as follows.

[The Talmudic statement that] "A person sees no flaw
within himself"[27] does not mean that a person is completely
unaware of his shortcomings. On the contrary, he may be
aware of and comprehend the depths of his deficiency even
more than another person. For someone else perceives only
what is visible to the eye, while he discerns what is in the
depths of his own heart.

The meaning, then, is that his fault is of no importance
to him, and therefore does not disturb him. It is as if he does
not see it at all, for his great self-love covers all his

---

26. *Ibid.* 22:21.
27. *Shabbat* 119a.

shortcomings.[28] Though intellectually aware of his deficiencies, he relegates them to a superficial, peripheral status, not allowing them to evoke a corresponding emotional feeling [of distress]. Accordingly, his shortcomings give him no cause to be concerned. Any fault becomes submerged in, and nullified by, his intense self-love and is dismissed to a state of latency.

Now, should another person perceive his fault, he is enraged, although he himself is well aware of it. Essentially, his anger is not aroused by the fact that the other person is mistaken in his judgment [suspecting him of a nonexistent defect]—for, indeed, he is aware of his shortcoming. Rather, the other person's perception of his defect renders it concrete and substantial, whereas when he alone knows of it, his self-love conceals it. He is angered that his friend revealed his flaw from its previously concealed and unfelt state (due to his self-love). But now, as far as his friend is concerned, it has become a definite and substantive shortcoming.

This, then [is what Hillel says], "what is hateful to you," namely, the revelation [of a shortcoming]—"do not do to your fellow"—do not perceive his faults and imperfections, whether in his social conduct or in his spiritual behavior, to consider them concrete and substantial. Instead, let your love for him be so great that it covers his flaw; do not permit the flaw to move from intellectual awareness to a negative emotional feeling.

When a person feels exceedingly great affection and goodwill for another, [a love] issuing from the very essence of

---

28. Cf. *Prov.* 10:12.

his soul, any wrong the other may inflict upon him will have no significance. It will be nullified in the great intensity of his love—"surging waters cannot extinguish the love . . ."[29]

Therefore, Hillel declared, "This is the whole Torah." For the complete unity of the souls of Israel, as if a single entity, evokes a most wondrous effect Above, which is the essence and purpose of the entire Torah. That is, the unity of the Holy One, blessed is He, with His *Shechinah*. His *Shechinah* is synonymous with *imma tata'ah* ("lower matriarch") and *matronita* ("matron"), the source of Jewish souls. "The beauty of Jacob was similar to Adam's," [state our Sages].[30] This means that Jacob, who incorporated all the souls, is akin to the beauty of *Adam haElyon* (the Supernal Being) upon His Throne, "the appearance of the likeness of G-d's Glory,"[31] for "His people is a part of the L-rd."[32]

When the souls of Israel join and unite, this in turn unites the *One* [G-d] with *one* [Israel]. That is, G-d becomes united with Israel. Once this union occurs, the Supernal Being sees no deficiency within Himself, and He removes every transgression of Israel, as "one who cleanses in the mighty ocean."[33] And as it is written, "He beholds no sin in Jacob and sees no wrongdoing in Israel"[34] for "the L-rd his G-d is with him;"[34]and Man does not see, metaphorically

---

29. *Songs* 8:7.
30. *Bava Metzia* 84a.
31. *Ezekiel* 1:26, 28.
32. *Deuteronomy*. 32:9.
33. Cf. *Zohar*, III, p. 132b.
34. *Numbers* 23:21.

speaking, his own fault. This should suffice for the intelligent.

The meaning of the phrase, "He beholds no . . . and sees no . . ." is not that they are concealed from Him, G-d forbid. For everything is revealed and known to Him, even one's trivial conversations.[35] Rather it means, as it says, "He sees iniquity but takes no notice of it."[36] The attribute of severity and judgment is not aroused by His infinite and boundless knowledge [of their wrong doings]. For His love covers it, as it is written, "And G-d (אלוה) screened for him."[37] אלוה (G-d) is a composite of אל-ו"ה which refers to the supernal kindness which encompasses, (and which is a garment of the soul and its seal), as is explained in *Etz Chaim*.

This is not the case, however, when, G-d forbid, the Jewish people are disunited. "Anyone who has within him a defect shall not approach to offer" and he causes, thereby, a disunity Above (between the Holy One, blessed is He, and the *Shechinah*, the Community of Israel). Then He will see the flaw, and that person's flaw in particular, for it was he who caused this disunity, Heaven forbid.

[The Divine blessings are contingent upon the unity of Israel, as we say in *Shemoneh Esrei*,] "Bless us, our Father, all of us as *one*"; with the result that, "You are wholly beautiful, My beloved, and there is no blemish in you."[38] This brings about the unity of the Holy One, blessed is He, with His

---

35. *Chagigah* 5b; *Kallah*, beg. ch. 3; *Vayikrah Rabbah* 26:7.
36. *Job* 11:11.
37. *Job* 3:23.
38. *Songs* 4:7.

Shechinah, i.e., the revelation of *Or Ein Sof* within the source of the souls of Israel to be "One with one."

This is the deeper meaning of the verse, "You shall be *tamim* (whole, perfect) with the L-rd your G-d."[39] G-d is in a state of completeness [and unity] with the totality of the souls of Israel. In other words, the radiance of the Supernal Wisdom [shines] into the totality of the parts of the *Shechinah*—[fulfilling] "You shall love your fellow as yourself," and does not behold his flaws. So, too, you shall be whole [and united] with your fellow so that the L-rd will be your G-d, through the offering of your self to G-d, in [the recital of the word] *Echad*, as has been discussed above.

This is why Hillel said "all the rest is but commentary." For, as is known, the purpose of all the *mitzvot* is to bring about the unity of the Holy One, blessed is He, with His *Shechinah*. Now, the essential unity of the Supernal Being with His *Shechinah*, called the *Beauty of Jacob*, depends upon the revelation of the true love, becoming actual self-love, for as mentioned above, "His people are part of G-d."

This is accomplished through the performance of the *mitzvah*, "You shall love your fellow as yourself," as explained above. All the other *mitzvot* are like a commentary that explains the unity.

(That is, in what form shall this unity take: whether an intellectual unity—man's wisdom with G-d's Wisdom—through Torah study, or an emotional unity of love or the other emotional attributes through the performance of the other *mitzvot*. As for example, if a person forms a strong

---

39. *Deuteronomy* 19:13.

bond of friendship with another, the cause of the attachment is true love.

The close relationship can take various forms: at times in speech, conversing upon intellectual matters; at times in emotion, displaying love for him; at times in deed, in doing him favors. Likewise, the 248 positive *mitzvot* correspond to the "248 organs of the King."[40] The performance of a specific *mitzvah* brings about the unity intrinsic to the particular organ [to which the *mitzvah* corresponds] and all the other attributes are contained within it. The same is the case in the performance of all other *mitzvot*).

For example, the *mitzvah* of wrapping oneself in the *tallit* [whose aim is to] "Accept upon yourself a King,"[41] [drawing over himself] the encompassing Light. This enables the recipient to offer his soul to G-d in [the recital of the word] *Echad*. For "if there is no fear [of G-d], there is no wisdom."[42] The fear which follows wisdom—as it is written, "If there is no wisdom there is no fear"—is complete self-abnegation which comes because of one's closeness to G-d. For the characteristic of fear is that as one comes closer, one is more overcome with a feeling of awe. The characteristic of love, on the other hand, is that the further one moves [from the object of his love], the stronger the love grows.

Accordingly, after a person has grasped the concept of His Oneness, he will be instilled with an awe of total self-surrender. And the vestige thereof becomes invested in the

40. *Tikkunei Zohar, Tikun* 30. V. *Tanya*, Part 1, ch. 23.
41. *Deuteronomy* 17, 15; See *Tanya*, Part 1, ch. 41.
42. *Avot* 3:7.

encompassing aspect of the *tallit,* inspiring him with an external fear that precedes wisdom.

All this is only an explanation of the unity generated by the soul's faculty of wisdom, when one offers his soul to G-d through [the recital of the word] *Echad.* This is the deeper meaning of unity, which essentially derives from the positive *mitzvah* of "Love your fellow . . ." For then, "*You are altogether beautiful, My beloved;*" and "*You shall be perfect with the L-rd your G-d,*" as explained above.

This *mitzvah* of "You shall love," and especially the negative precept, "You shall not hate . . ." can be explained from another perspective. That is, in light of the exposition, else-where,[43] on the verse, "Choose from among you . . . to bring the L-rd's retribution upon Midian."[44] There it explains that the *kelipah* of Midian is baseless hatred, and the retribution of G-d must be executed upon Midian. See there.

* * *

---

43. Rabbi Schneur Zalman of Liadi, *Likkutei Torah,* Vol. 3, p. 170 ff. [See also *On Ahavat Yisrael,* Kehot.]
44. *Number* 31:3.

Appendix

Sefer HaArachim–Chabad
Mitzvat Ahavat Yisrael

LOVE FOR A FELLOW JEW[1]

1. Definition

The *mitzvah* of *ahavat Yisrael*[2] obligates us to love every Jew, not only because he possesses virtues, a keen intellect or fine character traits, but because he is a Jew.[3] As such, *ahavat Yisrael* is predicated upon the soul of a Jew.

The love for another should be akin to the love for oneself, as it says,[4] "And you shall love your friend as yourself"—exactly "as yourself." Meaning, a person's love for his fellow Jew must be an intrinsic love, a love that transcends logic, just as—and identical to—one's own self-love. If one's own

---

1. [Only annotations appearing in square brackets are those of the translator; all others have been translated from the copious notes appearing in the original work, which contains many more references than have been translated in this English adaptation. When applicable, references in the original to Hebrew sources have been exchanged with references to English sources.]
2. Rambam, *Sefer HaMitvot*, command no. 206; Rambam, *Hilchot Dayot*, ch. 6, par. 3; *Chinuch*, command no. 243.
3. See *infra*, sect. 4, where it is explained that there must also be a love that is based on the other person's particular virtues.
4. *Lev.* 19:18.

personal affairs are of greater concern, then one has not yet
achieved true *ahavat Yisrael.*

Moreover, a person must cherish the other even more
than himself;[5] the needs of the other should concern him
more; and the suffering of the other ought to be more
distressing—may Heaven protect us. For a person can find
justification for his own misfortunes, but to do so for someone else—is absolutely impossible.[6]

To attain such love requires profound reflection. Such
reflection, though, serves only as a means to uncover this
innate love, a love that surpasses the very understanding that
reveals it. For *ahavat Yisrael* is a natural love, (not unlike the
love between brothers, or the love of a father for his son,)
which is engraved on every facet[7] of the soul.[8] The task,
therefore, is to awaken this love.

2. The Rationale for *Ahavat Yisrael*

Since people are distinct individuals, we would think
that their love would be based on logic, and limited by its
constraints. In truth, though, *ahavat Yisrael* is innate—for the
following reasons:

---

5. *HaYom Yom,* p. 26.
6. Hence, the true explanation of "love your friend as yourself" is not
    that one is bound to love one's friend as oneself. On the contrary,
    one is required to love *oneself* to the same extent that one loves
    another.
7. [Lit. "on every Jew's *neshamah, ruach,* and *nefesh.*" These refer to
    different levels or aspects of the soul. See *Tanya,* ch. 2, 3; *Midrash
    Rabbah* on *Gen.* 14:19.]
8. *HaYom Yom,* p. 49.

1. *Ahavat Yisrael* springs from a Jew's love of G-d, for one loves what his beloved loves.[9] Therefore, [since *ahavat HaShem* is innate to every Jew] *ahavat Yisrael* is [also] natural and innate to every Jew.

2. All Jews constitute particular components of a single whole, namely, the soul of *Adam HaRishon*, which was fragmented subsequently into a multitude of particular souls. Thus, every particular soul comprises within it all other particular souls. Consequently, one's fellow Jew is incorporated, spiritually, within oneself. Furthermore, from the perspective of their essential root, all souls form a single essence. When a single essence is divided into numerous parts, each part contains the entire essence.[10] A person's love for his fellow Jew, therefore, is not a love for another, but rather a love for oneself.

3. Achieving *Ahavat Yisrael*

Only by recognizing the primacy of the soul and the subordination of the body can one attain *ahavat Yisrael*. If a person regards his body as preeminent and his soul as ancillary, then he cannot possibly possess genuine *ahavat Yisrael*— only a conditional love, at best. For from a corporeal perspective, possessing disparate bodies, he and his friend are two distinct human beings. Thus for an essential love to exist between them is utterly impossible. Only he who despises and disdains his body [in and of itself] and who discerns the

---

9. See *infra*, sect. 6.
10. Consonant with the dictum of the Baal Shem Tov: An essence, when grasped in part, is grasped in its entirety.

primacy of his soul, can possess genuine *ahavat Yisrael*, an essential and unconditional love.[11]

Furthermore, even when an individual considers his soul to be preeminent, he can still not experience an essential love if he is mindful of his own distinct existence, though it be, admittedly, a purely spiritual one. Only when one's entire ego (*yeshus*) has been nullified can the quality of essence be revealed in a person—the singular essence common to every Jew. Then, because of the manifestation of the soul's essence, an essential love can flourish.

Though only possible when arising from the quintessence of the soul, as explained above, nonetheless, *ahavat Yisrael* arouses and reveals the soul's essence by a person cultivating and demonstrating this love. By identifying with the other, and shedding one's autonomous limitations, the essence of the soul is revealed.

4. Rational Love

To love every Jew with an essential love—because of the other's Jewishness—does not yet suffice. Recognizing the other's particular virtues, one should love him for rational reasons, as well.

Such virtues fall into one of two categories:

---

11. For this reason, *ahavat Yisrael* is analogous to *milah* (circumcision). *Orlah* (foreskin) symbolizes attachment to materialism. The idea of *milah* (removing the *orlah*) is to sever one's attachment to materialistic matters (so that one's involvement in all mundane pursuits is superficial), and to bind oneself to G-d's blessed unity. Since *ahavat Yisrael* is feasible only when worldly concerns are incidental to a person—"his soul is primary and his body secondary," the underlying concept of *ahavat Yisrael* is similar to that of *milah*.

1. Concealed virtues associated with the soul, since:

   a) "The soul and spirit, who can know their greatness and excellence in their root and source in the living G-d?"[12]

   b) Even if a person considers himself a "head" compared to his friend, his friend will always possess a quality, an aspect of perfection that he himself lacks. Thus, his own edification and perfection are consummated through his friend. For the perfection of the "head," too, is achieved specifically by the "feet," which are vital in carrying out its will.[13]

2. Visible virtues that are observable in all Jews, for example, love for simple Jews because of their very simplicity. For though unlettered, they believe in G-d and His Torah with perfect hearts. As for the scholars, one ought to love them because of their great erudition. For though very learned in Torah—which proves that their natural drives are stronger than the norm[14]—they are pious Jews all the same.[15] (This is aside from the inherent virtue in their Torah scholarship.) Thus, there is always a reason, a virtue for which, to love each Jew. Indeed, if a person cannot discern a virtue in his fellow that inspires this rational love, the deficiency lay not with the other, but with himself.

---

12. *Tanya*, ch. 32.
13. *Iggeret HaKodesh*, end of ch. 22.
14. See *Sucah* 52a.
15. Rabbi Y. Y. Schneersohn, *Likkutei Dibburim* (Eng. trans., Kehot, 1988), vol. 2, p. 105.

5. Boundless in Scope

Ahavat Yisrael must be boundless, and this should be evident in three areas. *First,* in the efforts one makes to foster the love, and in the favors one performs to benefit the other. *Second,* in those matters through which love and closeness are expressed. *Third,* in respect to the type of person who is loved (for love must be felt for all Jews equally).

(1) In Fostering the Love

Ahavat Yisrael demands exertion—one must toil in it tirelessly, using all of one's resourcefulness, comparable to a businessman in pursuit of his ventures. This exertion must be demonstrated:

a) in stimulating the love, which requires a person:

(a) to arouse himself *continuously* in *ahavat Yisrael,* to strive, with all of his heart and soul, to inculcate his heart with love for his fellow; to look favorably upon each and every Jew, regardless of who he may be; and to reflect on the other's virtues. This constitutes fulfillment of the command, "and you shall love your fellow like yourself." If an unsavory thought, concerning his friend should come to mind, he must drive it out as he would a thought concerning actual idolatry. (For in severity, slander is tantamount to idolatry, illicit sexual relations and murder.[16] And if sinful talk about one's fellow is so grave, how much more so are sinful thoughts. For thought, as is known, is far more potent than speech, in both its good effects and its negative ones). Furthermore,

---

16. *Arachin* 15b; *Tanchuma Metzorah* 2a.

the bad that a person sees in his friend may be only a projection of the bad within himself, and therefore, one should rather attribute the deficiency to oneself.

(b) to enlarge his circle of close friends and companions.

(c) to recount stories and anecdotes on the theme of fine character traits and *ahavat Yisrael* to his household at auspicious times, e.g., during *Shabbat* and *Yom Tov* meals.

b) in doing a favor for another, whether a material one or a spiritual one. (The degree of effort required here is comparable to that entailed by the servitude of a slave, viz., a person must *subjugate* himself to the other's welfare.)

And when, G-d forbid, news reaches him about the suffering of a Jew, be it physical suffering, or how much more so, spiritual suffering, a person must do all in his power to help him. He must do so without reservations (without considering, for example, his actual obligation). He must do so even when all of his efforts are of doubtful benefit— *perhaps* he can help. For the pain of another must pierce his soul's very core—and in the core of one's soul, there is no room for equivocation.

Indeed, when it comes to the pain of another, all considerations, even the principle, "the mind rules over the heart,"[17] must be negated. Not only must a person exert himself in all ways for another, but also he must likewise be prepared to act with self-sacrifice (even for a Jew whom he has never seen).[18] For *ahavat Yisrael* is similar to the love of G-d; hence, not only is one required to love one's fellow

---

17. *Tanya*, ch. 12.
18. *HaYom Yom*, p. 113.

"with all your heart, with all your soul,"[19] but also with— "all your might," which refers to—actual self-sacrifice.

(The meaning of "with all your heart," as it applies to *ahavat Yisrael*, is as follows. When two Jews meet, extending a greeting of *Shalom Aleichem* to one another, they should realize that their encounter occurs not only on a physical plane, a meeting of their two physical bodies, but also on a spiritual one. Namely, all five dimensions of their soul[20]— their *Nefesh*, *Ruach*, *Neshama*, *Chayah* and *Yechida*, embrace as well. When the above is kept in mind, then their *Shalom Aleichem* is truly *alive*. And the love referred to by the words, "with all your might" is the total self-sacrifice that one Jew possesses for another.)

In addition, *ahavat Yisrael* must be expressed not only by doing favors for one's fellow, but by behaving in a way that causes one's fellow to become beloved by others. For the love enjoined by the verse, "and you shall love your fellow as yourself,"[21] is comparable to that which is commanded by the verse, "and you shall love the L-rd your G-d."[22] Just as the latter verse intimates, "one must endear the Name of Heaven to others,"[23] so, too, does the former prescribe that one must endear his fellow to others.

---

19. *Deuteronomy* 6:5.
20. [See fn. 6.]
21. *Leviticus*. 19:18.
22. *Deuteronomy ibid*.
23. *Yomah* 86a.

(2) In Matters that Express Love and Closeness

The concerns of man are of two types: material—which revolve around the physical body, and spiritual—which revolve around the soul. *Ahavat Yisrael*, a feeling of affinity and unity with another, must be expressed in both areas. Unity should be demonstrated in material concerns (for example, a person should not suspect that the other would encroach on his domain). Since "his body is (ought to be) loathsome and despicable to him,"[24] matters of the body are of no consequence to him. Likewise, unity should be demonstrated in spiritual matters, concerns of the soul. For example, not to think that because of his own spiritual superiority, he cannot unite with his inferior, with someone who is altogether not his peer.

For, (a) "the soul and spirit, who can know their greatness and excellence in their root and source in the living G-d?"[25] Therefore, his fellow, in respect to his soul's root, may actually be *superior*, (b) "moreover, Jews are all alike, possessing the same Father";[26] consequently, all Jews are veritably "one."

Therefore, one's efforts for the welfare of another must be expressed both spiritually and materially. Occasionally, a soul descends to This World for a sojourn of 70 or 80 years in order to perform a single material favor, or particularly, a spiritual one, for a fellow Jew.[27]

* * *

---

24. *Tanya*, ch. 32.
25. *Tanya, ibid.*
26. *Tanya, ibid.*
27. A saying of the Baal Shem Tov, *Hayom Yom*, P. 51.

Aside from being an expression of *ahavat Yisrael* in and of itself, doing a person a material favor helps to bring him near spiritually. For having received a favor, he is aware of the material generosity of his benefactor. As such, "a debtor will not show a brazen face to his creditor."[28]

One of the methods in attracting a Jew to Torah and *mitzvot* is to help him (also) materially, and to do so without spiritual stipulations. Likewise, when rebuking another, even if about matters of the gravest concern, one must benefit him in some way first. Only then will reproach be accepted and bring about its desired effects.

For though *self-sacrifice* is demanded when striving to draw another closer to Judaism, this applies only to oneself. Concerning the other, however, disagreeable and divisive methods are forbidden (even) in order to draw him closer to Judaism. On the contrary, one must strive only to promote the other's welfare, as explained above.

(3) The Type of Jew who is to be Loved—All Jews Equally

One must love every Jew without exception, including one whom he has never met[29] (since an essential love applies even to a complete stranger), and one with whom, in a spiritual sense, he is utterly distant. Not only must one have *ahavat Yisrael* for a simple fellow, but one must possess the same love for an abject sinner as for a consummate *tzaddik*.[30]

Because *ahavat Yisrael* is an essential love, no distinctions are drawn between wicked and righteous. When a person

---

28. *Bava Metziah* 3a.
29. *HaYom Yom*, p. 25.
30. *Sefer HaSichot 5700*, p. 117.

perceives his own misdeeds, his self-love conceals them, as it says, "love masks all misdeeds."[31] The reason for this is because the love derives from the core of his soul, a level at which faults are of absolutely no consequence. So, too, with *ahavat Yisrael*, all of the other's vices, even those of the wicked, are veiled.

This is the meaning of what Hillel the Elder taught the convert: "What you detest, do not inflict upon your friend."[32] A person overlooks his own liabilities.[33] On the other hand, if another perceives his shortcomings as serious, then he is profoundly perturbed. So observing the dictum, ". . . do not inflict upon your friend," a person should ignore the other's failings and transgressions, because of his tremendous love for him.

For this reason, the wording of the directive, "One should love an incorrigible sinner just as one does a consummate *tzaddik*," falls short in conveying the true nature of *ahavat Yisrael*. For the phrase, ". . . an incorrigible sinner just as one does a consummate *tzaddik*," implies that there are various ranks. (Yet even so, one must still love an incorrigible sinner—yet only in a manner that approximates one's love for a consummate *tzaddik*—*just as*.) In truth, however, from the vantage point of an essential love, the spiritual state of another Jew is altogether irrelevant.

---

31. *Proverbs* 10:12.
32. *Shabbat* 31a.
33. Though aware of his shortcomings, he considers them utterly negligible; his faults are inundated and nullified by the immense love that conceal them.

Our Sages said that if one sees his companion sin, there is a *mitzvah* to hate him.[34] They intended this to apply, however, only when the other is his companion, his peer, in the study of Torah and the observance of *mitzvot*. It further only applies after one has duly fulfilled one's obligation in properly admonishing the person,[35] but he has still not forsaken his sin. However, if the fellow is neither one's peer nor one's friend, then, on the contrary, one must attract him with strong cords of love. For with such an approach, there may be a chance in bringing him near to the Torah and the service of G-d.[36]

The obligation to try to draw another Jew to the service of G-d applies to all types of Jews. It pertains to those Jews who can be likened metaphorically to a barren desert, being vacant and void of all virtues. They possess neither Torah learning, nor wisdom, nor commendable character traits—they lack even simple civility—to the point that they lack any trace of humanity. [Yet, such Jews must also be loved.] For regarding even "creatures"—those who possess no virtues whatsoever, and who can be considered to be mere creatures (i.e., their whole virtue is that they are creations of the Holy One blessed be He)[37]—we are commanded,[38] "Be of the disciples of Aaron . . . loving your fellow *creatures*, and bringing them near to Torah." Indeed, efforts in this regard are effective even when dealing with those who claim to be

---

34. See *Peshachim* 113b, *Arachin* 16b.
35. Leviticus 19:17.
36. *Tanya, ibid.*
37. See *Taanit* 20b.
38. *Avot* 1:12.

non-believers. Moreover, "we are assured by covenant that any wide-ranging effort and labor shall never be fruitless."[39]

The above obligation [to draw another Jew to the service of G-d] applies also to those Jews who can be metaphorically likened to an ocean. Such Jews find themselves at the extreme end of the spectrum in the vastness of their knowledge: brimming and over-flowing with the waters of Torah—yet deficient, all the same, in their fear of G-d.

These people, too, must be brought near to the service of G-d through *ahavat Yisrael*. For although their Torah learning may have failed to awaken in them the fear of G-d, *ahavat Yisrael* that stems from the soul's core[40] can still succeed in stimulating a fear of G-d in them, by arousing the core of their soul.

If, after all, a person fails to bring the other closer to Torah and *mitzvot*, nonetheless, he does not forfeit the reward for showing love to a fellow Jew.[41]

Furthermore, even when there is a *mitzvah* to hate some-one—a close friend who has not repented after being rebuked—there is still a *mitzvah* to love him, as well. For the hatred is evinced (only) because of the evil within him. However, because of his hidden goodness (i.e., the spark of G-dliness that enlivens his G-dly soul), there is a *mitzvah* to love him. In addition, one must awaken compassion for his friend's divine soul, which is exiled in the evil within him, for compassion extinguishes hatred, and kindles love in its stead.

---

39. *HaYom Yom*, p. 31 [p. 95.]
40. Of the one who loves them, as explained above, sect. 3.
41. *Tanya, ibid.*

In addition to all the above, for two reasons one must reach out even to heretics and atheists. These are people about whom King David writes,[42] "With a consummate hatred, I hate them"[43] (since they have no portion in the G-d of Israel)[44]:

(a) Regarding these people, too, the verse says,[45] "Sin will be excised,"—*sin*, but not sinners.[46] Consequently, one must try to bring them near and rehabilitate them, to ensure that sin will be excised, not the sinners themselves.

(b) Nowadays heresy stems for the most part from a lack of knowledge.[47] Besides which, faith (and its antithesis— denial) is ultimately a matter of the heart, and what lies in the heart of another, no one can truly know.[48]

The other may espouse and practice heresy (and a Jewish court of law [in the past] would be compelled to punish such behavior, for "men see with their eyes"[49]). Yet, it is still plausible that in the heart of hearts, the scoffer actually believes. In light of this possibility, one is obliged, here too, to "judge every person favorably."[50]

* * *

For this reason, Rabbi Yosef Yitzchak Schneersohn of Lubavitch was accustomed to reaching out to *all* Jews, even

---

42. *Shabbat* 116a.
43. *Psalms* 139:22.
44. *Tanya, ibid.*
45. *Psalms* 104:35.
46. *Berachot* 10a.
47. *Sefer HaMa'amarim 5711*, P. 242.
48. *Pesachim* 54b.
49. *Samuel* I, 16:7.
50. *Avot* 1:6.

to those about whom it says, "We precipitate their downfall, and do not come to their aid."[51] When questioned about his conduct, his apparent disregard for the law pertaining to such scoundrels, and his persistence in reaching out to them, he replied:

> The *Shulchan Aruch* comprises four volumes, of which *Choshen Mishpat* is the *fourth*. In this volume itself, there are over 420 sections. The details of the laws governing those who might deserve such a verdict are found in the very *last* sections of *Choshen Mishpat*.
>
> Only after one has studied and complied with all the laws from the beginning of *Orach Chaim*, [the first volume] until these concluding ones, may one presume to rule on these regulations.

In other words, if a person behaves cruelly towards a fellow Jew, claiming that the Torah sanctions such behavior, it is possible (aside from perhaps misinterpreting the *halacha*) that he is really motivated by something else. Perhaps his behavior is fueled by his own bad temperament, despite his rationalization that his conduct is prompted by his fear of G-d. In contrast, when a person does a favor for another, there is no doubt whatsoever that a *mitzvah* has been performed.

---

51. [*Avodah Zarah* 26b; *Shulchan Aruch, Choshen Mishpat*, sect. 425.]

6. Its Relationship to *Ahavat HaShem* and *Ahavat HaTorah*

Ahavat HaShem, *ahavat HaTorah*, and *ahavat Yisrael* are one, like a singular essence; therefore, each of these loves contains all the others. For an essence, when grasped in part, is grasped in its entirety.

For this reason, *ahavat Yisrael*:

1. acts as a barometer for one's love of G-d. When *ahavat Yisrael* is wanting, this indicates that one's *ahavat HaShem* is also deficient (and will not be sustained). For if a father is truly loved, then so are his children.[52]

2. contains (within *itself*—and clarifies and elucidates) *ahavat HaShem*, for a Jew is truly "a part of G-d above."[53] By loving another Jew—a part of G-d—one thereby loves G-d Himself.[54]

3. serves as a vehicle to attaining *ahavat HaShem*.[55] *Ahavat HaShem* (and *ahavat HaTorah*) can be achieved eventually by means of *ahavat Yisrael* (even though *ahavat Yisrael* is a rational precept dictated by logic). In addition, by laboring on *ahavat Yisrael*, a person merits to attain a loftier level in *ahavat HaShem*. Should one happen to meet an individual who possesses only *ahavat Yisrael*, one must try to change him. That is, one should try (a) to bring him to *ahavat HaTorah* and *ahavat HaShem*, (b) so that his

---

52. *HaYom Yom*, p. 81.
53. *Tanya*, beg. ch. 2.
54. *HaYom Yom*, p. 78.
55. *On Ahavat Yisrael*, p. 101; *HaYom Yom*, p. 93.

ahavat Yisrael is expressed not only by giving food to the famished and water to the parched, but also by bringing other Jews near to ahavat HaTorah and ahavat HaShem, prompted by his own ahavat Yisrael.

* * *

Of these three loves, ahavat Yisrael ranks supreme, as the others are incorporated within it. Where there is ahavat Yisrael, there is ahavat HaTorah and ahavat HaShem. In contrast, ahavat HaShem does not necessarily lead to ahavat HaTorah, nor ahavat HaTorah, to ahavat Yisrael.

That ahavat Yisrael surpasses ahavat HaShem can readily be inferred from the verse, "I loved you, said the L-rd."[56] Ahavat Yisrael is thus preeminent, since by loving a fellow Jew, a person loves the one whom his beloved loves.[57]

In his divine service, a person progresses from ahavat Yisrael to ahavat HaTorah, and then, to ahavat HaShem.

These three loves correspond to the three pillars upon which the world stands: Torah, prayer, and charitable deeds.[58] Ahavat Yisrael corresponds to charitable deeds; ahavat HaTorah, to Torah; and ahavat HaShem, to prayer.

7. The Supernal Effects of Ahavat Yisrael

Ahavat Yisrael exercises a profound influence on the emanations and affects from On High in several respects:

---

56. Malachi 1:2.
57. HaYom Yom, p. 49.
58. Avot 1:2.

1. It affects the flow and unity of the *Ein Sof*-light with *Knesset Yisrael*.[59] Only when the Jewish people are one, when they have merged into a single entity, does the Oneness of G-d rest upon them. This is not the case, however, when there is divisiveness, Heaven forbid. (Namely, when individuals are estranged from one another, each asserting,[60] "What is mine, is mine. . . ." For when the Jewish people are polarized, the Oneness of G-d's unity does not rest upon them.) *Knesset Yisrael* then becomes disunited from G-d, since "the Holy One, blessed be He, does not dwell in a defective place."[61]

2. The Almighty overlooks the liabilities of the Jewish people. Although their shortcomings are not actually concealed from Him, Heaven forbid, they appear utterly insignificant. As the verse says, "He sees no iniquity in Israel."[62] For through *ahavat Yisrael*, G-d unites with the Jewish people, becoming as one, as explained above. When so united,[63] "(Supernal) Man[64] takes no notice of *his own* deficiency." Conversely, when one despises another Jew, G-d is then separated from *Knesset Yisrael*, as explained above. G-d

---

59. This unification is also referred to as the unity of the Holy One blessed be He with the *Shechinah*, as the *Shechinah* is the source of Jewish souls.
60. *Avot* 5:10.
61. *Zohar* III 90b.
62. *Num.* 23:21.
63. [*Shabbat* 119a.]
64. [Just as man ignores his own shortcomings, so too when a Jew is united with Supernal Man, an allusion to the G-d-head, G-d ignores a Jew's shortcoming. For when so united, any shortcoming of man's is considered by Him to be as His own, as it were.]

then notices the faults of the Jewish people, in general, and of the one possessing the hatred in particular, since it was he who instigated the discord.

3. G-d fulfills the petitions of the Jewish people, his children. When a father sees his children interacting with fraternal love, peace and harmony, each child as concerned about the other's welfare as he is about his own—some actually putting aside their own cares to tend to those of their siblings—then pleased and delighted by his children's behavior, the father strives to fulfill their requests.

Therefore:

> a) The blessings that one wishes his fellow arouses G-d's mercy, and is more effective in doing so than the appeals and entreaties by Micha'el, the Angel of Mercy.[65]
>
> b) The sigh of one Jew over the other's misfortune breaches the iron barriers erected by the accusations of any celestial prosecutors. Similarly, the joy of one Jew, and his blessing over the other's good fortune are as cherished by G-d as the prayer of R. Yochanan the High Priest in the Holy of Holies.

4. The bounty emanating from Above is strongly influenced by one's fulfillment of the *mitzvah* of *ahavat Yisrael*. When one loves a fellow Jew, one is loved by G-d; when one does another a favor, one obtains favor from G-d; and when one reaches out to another, G-d reaches out to him. As a reward for his benevolence (even in material matters) to any

---

65. Especially at a Chasidic gathering.

Jew—for concerning every Jew, the verse says, "I loved you, said the L-rd,"[66] indicating that G-d's love for every Jew is comparable to a parent's love for an only child—G-d repays him many times over.

5. Through self-sacrifice for *ahavat Yisrael*, one merits the revelation of the dimension of the soul called *Mah*.[67] *Ahavat Yisrael* is more efficacious in revealing this level than the most profound comprehension of G-dliness and dedicated service to Him. For the *Mah* within those who lack *ahavat Yisrael* may possibly be lost, Heaven forbid. In contrast, those who involve themselves in *ahavat Yisrael* with self-sacrifice can be confident of sustaining their spiritual standing; moreover, they "return the (spiritual) losses of others to their owners."[68]

6. *Ahavat Yisrael* will secure the future redemption,[69] since it counteracts the baseless hatred (שנאת חנם) that was the cause of exile in the first place.[70] Therefore, it is through *ahavat Yisrael*—unconditional love (אהבת חנם), love also for those who possess no discernible virtue, and for those who are "free from *mitzvot*"[71]—(the very opposite of "*baseless* hatred") that the redemption will come about.

---

66. *Malachi* 1:2.
67. [See Rabbi Y. Y. Schneersohn, *Chassidic Discourses* (Eng. trans., Kehot, N.Y., 1986), Vol. 2, p. 406 *et passim*.]
68. *Likkutei Sichot* (Eng. trans., Kehot, N.Y., 1980), vol. I, p. 205.
69. *Tanchuma, Netzavim* 1b, "The Jewish people will not be redeemed until they stand united as a single group."
70. *Yoma* 9b.
71. *Sifri, Num.* 11:5.

8. The Foundation of the Entire Torah

Ahavat Yisrael is the foundation of the entire Torah, and is its underlying fundamental principle.[72] Therefore, one should not be lax, Heaven forbid, in its observance, as such laxity makes room for excessive leniency with all *mitzvot*, G-d forbid. On the contrary, from other *mitzvot*, it can be deduced *a fortiori* that *ahavat Yisrael* should be observed most vigorously.[73] Indeed, the first *mitzvah* in the Torah, be fruitful and multiply, is really one of *ahavat Yisrael*, as it commands every Jew to try to create another.

The reasons for this are the following:

1. The foundation and root of the whole Torah is to raise and elevate the soul above the body, a concept that finds expression in *ahavat Yisrael*. (As explained above in ch. 3, genuine *ahavat Yisrael* is possible only for a person who considers his soul to be paramount, and his body, subordinate).[74]

2. The foundation and root of the whole Torah is to elicit the blessed *Ein Sof*-light into *Knesset Yisrael* (the unification of the Holy One, blessed be He, and His *Shechinah*). This bond is accomplished through *ahavat Yisrael* (as explained above, ch. 7).

3. The foundation of the Torah is identified with the World of *Tikun*, which is characterized by the quality of mutual inclusion. *Ahavat Yisrael*, too, is based on the concept of mutual inclusion (each person should view himself as being incorporated within the other).

---

72. *Shabbat* 31a; see also *Yerushalmi, Nedarim* 9:4, "And you shall love your fellow as yourself... this is a major Torah principle."
73. *Likkutei Sichot, ibid.*, p. 37.
74. *Tanya*, ch. 32.

Hence the [first part of the] dictum, "Love your fellow Jew as yourself . . ."—(is predicated on the concept of) mutual inclusion, which also characterizes *Tikun*, the foundation of Torah. The dictum thus concludes, ". . . this [concept of mutual incorporation, a concept promulgated by the *mitzvah* of *ahavat Yisrael*] is [identical to that which underlies] the entire Torah."

This is the meaning of what our Sages said, "This is the entire Torah; the rest is but commentary."[75] Since,

1) The whole goal of *mitzvot* is that a person reaches this level—a level where he is no longer bound to matters of This World, a level where his sole ambition is G-d's blessed Unity. Moreover, it is precisely this spiritual perspective that the *mitzvah* of *ahavat Yisrael* demands, as explained earlier.

2) The unification of G-d and the *Shechinah* is achieved principally through *ahavat Yisrael,* as explained above. All the other *mitzvot* are but like a "commentary" to *explain* the unity—how to bring about the unification. For every *mitzvah* constitutes a different path to accomplishing this unity.

3) Through *ahavat Yisrael*, the unification and mutual inclusion of *Tikun* is accomplished in a broad way. The other *mitzvot* constitute the specific unifications of *Tikun*.

9. A Fundamental Principle of Chasidus in Particular

Ahavat Yisrael is one of the fundamental principles of Chasidic ideology.[76] (In *Tanya*, the "Written Law" of Chabad Chasidus, wherever one turns, the phenomenal *ahavat Yisrael* of the Alter Rebbe, its author, is apparent. Moreover, a

---

75. *Shabbat* 31a.
76. *HaYom Yom*, p. 77.

whole chapter in *Tanya* is dedicated to this subject: Chapter 32 (לב), which indicates that this chapter is the heart (לב) of the entire work.[77])

Therefore, a Chasid is one who devotes himself to pursuing the other's welfare. He willingly forgoes his own betterment for the sake of someone else's, and does so even when his own benefit would be certain, while the other's is only doubtful.

To illustrate the extent to which the concept of *ahavat Yisrael* is demanded by Chasidic doctrine: In the days of the Alter Rebbe the love among Chasidim had surpassed the love between brothers. So much so, outsiders would often express their earnest wish that the love between brothers in their fold be as deep as the love among Chasidim. Nonetheless, the Alter Rebbe declared that even the love of these Chasidim did not *at all* reach the *ahavat Yisrael* desired by the Baal Shem Tov.

In view of their demands of those who would follow their example concerning *ahavat Yisrael*, the *Rebbeim* disclosed several incidents regarding their own conduct in this matter, in order to facilitate compliance with their expectations.[78]

* * *

In Chasidic philosophy, there is a difference between the *ahavat Yisrael* as taught by the Baal Shem Tov, the Maggid of Mezhirech, and the Alter Rebbe (and his successors). It was

---

77. [See R. Nissan Mindel's Introduction to Part I of *Tanya* (bi-lingual ed., Kehot, N.Y.) p. 839.]

78. Rabbi Y. Y. Schneersohn and Rabbi Menachem M. Schneerson, *Basi LeGani, Chassidic Discourses* (Eng. trans., Kehot, N.Y., 1990) pp. 96-97.

the Baal Shem Tov who revealed the idea that *ahavat HaShem*, *ahavat HaTorah* and *ahavat Yisrael* are interconnected. The Maggid, in turn, revealed the *comprehension* underlying the connection between these three loves. He did so by providing a profound explanation of the three sorts of love referred to by the verse, "with all your heart, with all your soul, and with all your might."[79] Finally, the Alter Rebbe revealed how every individual is *able, required and compelled* to bring these three loves to fruition. He stated that *ahavat Yisrael* is the supernal gate[80] on which luminous words are engraved, declaring: "This is the gateway to Above."

Thus, though *ahavat Yisrael* is common to all Jews, particularly to those in Chasidic circles, the *ahavat Yisrael* of Chabad Chasidim ought to be rivaled by none.

* * *

Some reasons why *ahavat Yisrael* is interwoven with Chasidic philosophy:

Doing someone a material favor expresses the unity between the material and spiritual. For the material welfare of one person becomes the spiritual concern of the second. As such, it is an expression of the unity of G-d, which is one of the principle themes of Chasidic ideology.

Ahavat Yisrael hastens the future redemption;[81] similarly, Chasidic philosophy [and its dissemination]—"when your

---

79. *Deuteronomy* 6:5.
80. See also *Likkutei Dibburim*, *ibid.*, p. 104, "The Baal Shem Tov . . . taught that *ahavat Yisrael* is the first gate that grants one entry into the courtyards of G-d."
81. As explained above, at the end of sect. 7.

wellsprings are spread abroad"[82]—prepares the world for the arrival of *Mashiach*.[83]

10. A Preparation for *Matan Torah*

On the verse, "Israel camped opposite the mountain,"[84] our Sages noted the unusual singular form of the verb 'camped,' and commented, "As a single person, with a single heart."[85]

Ahavat Yisrael was a preparation to *Matan Torah* for the following reasons:

Ahavat Yisrael arouses the soul's essence,[86] and *Matan Torah*, a phenomenon originating in the essence of the blessed *Ein Sof*, targeted and affected the essence of the Jewish soul.

The entire Torah was given to promote peace in the world;[87] therefore, a state of peace and unity was also the logical preparation and conduit for *Matan Torah*.

---

82. [Cf. *Proverbs* 5:16; this was the *Mashiach's* reply to the Baal Shem Tov's question as to when he, the *Mashiach*, would come to usher in the final redemption. See following fn.]

83. [For the source, see Rabbi Menachem M. Schneerson, *On the Essence of Chassidus* (Eng. trans., Kehot, N.Y., 1978), p. 15, fn. 23; also, Rabbi Immanuel Schochet, *The Mystical Dimension* (Kehot, N.Y., 1990), vol. 1, pp. 120-121; see also *Likkutei Dibburim*, ibid., p. 227.]

84. *Exodus* 19:2.

85. *Mechilta, ad loc.*; *Rashi, ad loc.*

86. As explained at the end of sect. 3.

87. *Rambam*, "Laws of Chanuka," near the end; see also the *Sifri* on *Numbers* 6:26.

11. A Preparation for Tefillah[88]

"Before prayer, it is proper to declare: I hereby take upon myself to fulfill the command, *Love your fellow man as yourself*."[89] This acceptance, in which a person includes himself in the prayer of Israel as a whole, represents the true ideal of communal prayer.

In explaining the connection between one's preparedness to fulfill the precept of *ahavat Yisrael*, and the act of prayer itself, several salient points need to be considered:

1. *Ahavat Yisrael* serves as the gateway through which a person can approach G-d in prayer.[90]

2. It serves as a preparation to the purification and sacrifice of the animalistic soul during prayer. For "And you shall love your friend as yourself" requires that *Tohu*[91] be purified to resemble *Tikun*.[92] For *Tohu* and *Tikun* are referred to as "friends." And by accepting upon oneself the *mitzvah* enjoined by the verse, "And you shall love your friend as yourself"—which involves the purification of *Tohu* (the

---

88. See also *Bava Batra* 10a.
89. Rabbi Schneur Zalman of Liadi, *Siddur, Tehillat Hashem* (Eng. trans., Kehot, N.Y., 1988), p. 12.
90. *HaYom Yom*, p. 67.
91. [Lit. "chaos." See fn. *infra*.]
92. [Lit. "correction." *Tohu* and *Tikun* refer to two different schemes through which divinity is manifest in creation. An over-abundance of Light and a paucity of suitable receptacles to contain it characterize the first. In the second scheme, one whose purpose was to provide a framework in which to rectify the "damage" of the first, the Light is not as abundant. The vessels channeling the Light are able to contain it successfully. See R. Immanuel Schochet's, *Mystical Concepts in Chassidism*, published in *Tanya* (bi-lingual ed., Kehot, NY, 1973) p. 876.]

source of the animal soul), the animal soul is given the capacity to be purified and elevated through prayer.

Concerning the sacrificial offerings, it was necessary for man (*Adam*, whose numerical value is 45) to first lay his hands upon the animal (*behema*, whose numerical value is 52) *before* its sacrifice. This was required in order to endow it with the capacity to be elevated through its subsequent offering. So, too, *before* the offering of the *animal* soul, before prayer (prayers having been instituted to correspond to the daily sacrifices),[93] the animal soul has to be given the power to be elevated. This is accomplished through accepting upon oneself the *mitzvah* of *ahavat Yisrael*.

3. It prepares a person for the elevation that occurs during prayer in the following ways:

(a) Every soul incorporates within it [an aspect of] all other souls.[94] Therefore, when a person despises another Jew, he severs his own soul from an aspect of the other's soul that was originally included within himself.

Consequently, the person is blemished, since he is now missing this particular aspect. In this imperfect state, he cannot ascend [spiritually through prayer] to find favor before G-d. For the blessed *Ein Sof*-light is all-encompassing, and as such, cannot tolerate a person who is defective, who is missing a [spiritual] aspect of another [on account of his own hatred].

Only through *ahavat Yisrael*, when the coalescence of his soul with all souls is intact, when his soul is thus healthy and

---

93. *Berachot* 26a.
94. As explained above in sect. 2.

complete, can a person ascend and find favor before G-d, Who Himself embraces all.

(b) Prayer elevates a person, enabling him to fulfill [the spiritual demands of] the precept of *Kriat Shema*, i.e., to love G-d. And *ahavat Yisrael* is a vehicle to achieving *ahavat HaShem*.[95]

(c) During the ascent engendered by prayer, a person is bidden to elevate even the lowest levels external to himself. If he fails to do so, then his own ascent is jeopardized.

Therefore, prior to prayer, a person must unite with all Jewish people, including the lowest and least worthy members among them—wherever these people live—despite their being complete strangers—and regardless of their radically lower stature.

4. *Ahavat Yisrael* prepares for the elicitation and acceptance of the lofty revelations that are revealed during prayer. For when a person lovingly performs a favor for another Jew, (1) the gates to the supernal palaces are opened before him[96] (the Divine bounty is elicited), (2) his mind and heart become receptive to the revelations.

5. *Ahavat Yisrael* ensures that one's prayer will be established firmly, that it will not wane. Otherwise, if one segregates oneself from others, and one's divine service is typified by a single characteristic,[97] the impure forces may derive vitality from his worship. Only by merging with all

---

95. As explained above in sect. 6.
96. *HaYom Yom*, p. 66.
97. [I.e., a single dominant emotive-trait characterizes his service, since every individual soul is rooted in a particular *Sefirah*; cf. *Tanya*, Compiler's Foreword, pp. 3b, 4a; also, *Iggeret HaKodesh*, ch. 13.]

the Jewish people, who collectively serve G-d in a middle path, can a person's service enjoy strong continuity, without indirectly nourishing the impure forces.

6. *Ahavat Yisrael* helps to ensure that one's petitions during prayer are fulfilled.[98] For *ahavat Yisrael* gives G-d gratification, and because of this gratification, G-d fulfills the worshipper's request.[99]

12. Was a Preparation for the Construction of the *Mishkan*

Before the *Mishkan* was built, the Jewish people had to be imbued with *ahavat Yisrael*; they had to unite and become a single entity. Accordingly, (a) it was necessary to "assemble" the Jewish people, as the verse describes, "Moshe *assembled* the *entire* Israelite community"[100] (to convey to them G-d's command concerning their contributions towards the *Mishkan's* construction). They had to become a single "community." (b) The construction of the *Mishkan* had to be carried out through Betzalel, of the tribe of Yehudah, and through Oholiav, of the tribe of Dan, viz., through representation from both the most noble tribe, and the most lowly.

The construction of the *Mishkan* was contingent upon *ahavat Yisrael* for the following reasons:

a) The command, "They shall make Me a sanctuary," was for the purpose of "and I will dwell among them."[101]

---

98. *HaYom Yom*, p. 67.
99. As explained above in sect. 7.
100. *Num.* 35:1.
101. *Num.* 25:8.

In other words, for the purpose of drawing down [revealing in this world] G-d's Essence, His simple Unity.

This drawing down is accomplished through, "Moshe assembled," i.e., through *ahavat Yisrael*, and the Jewish people uniting as one, in all respects, in both material matters and spiritual ones.

b) The goal in building the *Mishkan* was to elevate base material items and transform them into vehicles for G-dliness; therefore, the *Mishkan* was built out of physical substances, "gold and silver. . . ."

The objective, then, was similar to that of prayer, i.e., to elevate even the lowliest forms of existence.[102] Accordingly, it was necessary for the most lowly of the tribes to participate in the *Mishkan's* construction.

This is analogous to prayer, before which a person must identify himself with the lowliest members of the Jewish people. He does so with the goal of elevating them, afterwards, through his prayer.

---

102. As explained above in sect. 11.

הוצאת ספרים

קרני הוד תורה

קה״ת

ליובאוויטש